MANIFESTING YOUR DREAMS

ENCOURAGEMENT FOR PEOPLE WHO DON'T HAVE ENOUGH

ALAN RAMSEY, DTM

outskirts
press

Manifesting Your Dreams
Encouragement For People Who Don't Have Enough
All Rights Reserved.
Copyright © 2017 Alan Ramsey, DTM
v2.0

The opinions expressed in this manuscript are solely the opinions of the author and do not represent the opinions or thoughts of the publisher. The author has represented and warranted full ownership and/or legal right to publish all the materials in this book.

This book may not be reproduced, transmitted, or stored in whole or in part by any means, including graphic, electronic, or mechanical without the express written consent of the publisher except in the case of brief quotations embodied in critical articles and reviews.

Outskirts Press, Inc.
http://www.outskirtspress.com

Paperback ISBN: 978-1-4787-7979-7

Cover Image by Alan Ramsey, DTM

Outskirts Press and the "OP" logo are trademarks belonging to Outskirts Press, Inc.

PRINTED IN THE UNITED STATES OF AMERICA

TABLE OF CONTENTS

Chapter 1:	The Power of Passion	1
Chapter 2:	Overcoming Your Fears	4
Chapter 3:	Seeds of Ideas	8
Chapter 4:	Beating the Odds	11
Chapter 5:	Surviving Dream Storms	14
Chapter 6:	Dream Anchors	17
Chapter 7:	Olympic Dream Moments	22
Chapter 8:	Live Your Dreams	27
Chapter 9:	Dream Fighters	30
Chapter 10:	Dream Your Way Out!	33
Chapter 11:	Dream Contenders vs. Dream Pretenders	36

Chapter 12:	Dream Pearls	39
Chapter 13:	Dream Diamonds	42
Chapter 14:	Opportunities of Gold	45
Chapter 15:	Dream Merchants	48
Chapter 16:	Dream Builders	52
Chapter 17:	Exercising Dream Options	57
Chapter 18:	Dream Comebacks	60
Chapter 19:	Dream Champions	63
Chapter 20:	Dream Investors	66
Chapter 21:	Building Your Dream Team	69

Chapter 1

THE POWER OF PASSION

Passion brings focus and clarity to our dreams.

When we look through the right lens (passion), we can focus on the clarity of our dreams. During a recent trip to the optometrist, I was given an eye exam and the doctor asked me, "Which lens is clearer, one or two?" Your passion lens takes you closer to your dream and brings your dream closer to you. It brings definition and clarity to what you are looking at, both up close and far away. When you see your dreams clearly through your passion lens, you no longer have to guess at what you should be doing.

People do strange things when they have a passion to experience something in life. On Black Friday, people will wait in long lines for hours or even camp out overnight to purchase a flat-screen TV, laptop computer, iPad, or a plethora of other products at a bargain price. One of my dreams was to see Debbye Turner once she became Miss America, so I took off from work and went to the parade and stood in a large crowd of people just for the opportunity to see her ride by in a convertible and wave to the crowd. This is a moment, I will never forget. I don't particularly care for crowds, but my passion overrode my fears and allowed me to step outside my comfort zone. Our passion will take us places where we would not normally go.

Passion is a fuel that energizes your actions to get you going. It's like the adrenaline when you run in a race to reach the finish line. Passion is invigorating, rejuvenating and motivating. Passion is a powerful emotion that causes you to take action.

What things are you passionate about in life? One of my passions is vacationing on cruise ships. When I was young, I drew pictures of yachts. This childhood dream blossomed into traveling on cruise ships as well as assisting others in planning and experiencing their dream vacations. As a child I, saw it as a small thing, but as I grew older, the passion lens brought clarity and focus to the fulfillment of the dream. My first business launch was Destinations Cruise Agency. My theme was "Cruising Destinations to Paradise." For me, this was a hobby, but it was also my passion.

I continued to operate this business out of my home while working a full-time job. In 2002, my regular job downsized and I was released from the payroll. At that point, everything went into survival mode, and as a result I was forced to shut down the home business. Years later, I would meet former clients in public who inquired about my travel business. I came to the realization that I was missing opportunities because I was not positioned to receive their business. In 2007, I attended a *Power*Networking conference and discovered a business opportunity in travel, so I signed up with InteleTravel and became an Independent Travel Agent. This venture gives me the opportunity to experience my travel dreams as well as assist others in realizing their travel dreams. Passion is the power that makes dreams fly.

Chapter 2

Overcoming Your Fears

Face your fears by fueling your dreams.

Don't be afraid to dream.

Don't be afraid to fly.

Don't be afraid to swim.

Don't be afraid to try.

What are you afraid of, anyway? Is it success or failure? The best way to overcome your fears is to confront them. Fears prevent us from going places and doing things in life we were created to experience.

For example, some people never go on cruises because they fear the water. I've often heard people say, "I'm not going to drown in all of that water." My perspective is that there is so much water out there that it has to keep me afloat. Early on in life, I learned not to fear water. I am not a good swimmer, but I was never afraid to experience the adventure of jumping off of the diving board into deep water and then finding a way to make it safely to the side of the pool. In water, we must obey the laws of buoyancy and float with the water and resist the urge to fight against it.

I don't feel comfortable flying but have found it necessary in order to realize some of my travel dreams. Once the plane leaves the runway and the laws of aerodynamics take over, you are at the mercy of the plane and the pilot to get you safely to your destination. Then, there's this phenomenon called *turbulence* that you may experience along the way. Flying is an adventure in itself. You get to experience another world high above the clouds. Looking down, you get to see how small things that were once tall buildings, freeways, acres of land and rivers really are.

I once lived near Hartsfield-Jackson Atlanta International Airport and was quite intrigued by watching the planes as they came in and out of the airport. Each plane has its departure time, arrival time and destination. Flying is not my preferred mode of travel, but if the need arises, I face this fear, rise to the occasion and soar.

The first thing fear does is limit our opportunities. People who don't fly will never see places that are far away. Those who choose not to get into the water will never learn to float and swim. Individuals who never move out of their comfort zones will never experience the greatness of their true potential. Face your fears and they will disappear. Fuel your dreams and they will manifest your true potential.

Secondly, fear places boundaries around our dreams. We have thoughts like, "This is as much as I can do or as far as I can go." A fear boundary will prevent you from manifesting your dreams because you are afraid to move beyond a certain point. It's like living in the city of Atlanta and never going outside of I-285, which circles around the city. If my dream destination is outside the perimeter, I must not allow the interstate to be a boundary that prevents me from leaving.

The stronghold of fear set up in the mind limits our thoughts and behavior. It reduces options and limits the dream.

I'm afraid to go there because...

Some years ago, there was some fear around the town of Cumming, Georgia because of tense racial relations. I had a friend and co-worker who lived there invite me to visit. I was somewhat hesitant about going because of the negative publicity the town had received. I overcame my fear by going and experienced a nice town with nice people. On each trip, I explain to them that I will be on the road home before sunset.

The third thing fear does is create barriers. Unlike boundaries, which are designed to keep you in places, barriers are designed to keep you out of places. It's like a roadblock or the yellow police tape at a crime scene. When we envision a present threat or danger as real, we avoid going certain places or attempting to do certain things. When we have fears of failing at something, we are often hesitant in even trying. Real failure is not in not succeeding, but in not trying.

Failures are the stepping-stones and building blocks to success. It's like learning to skate for the first time; we must fall down before we can skate with proficiency. Even the best figure skaters fall when they succumb to the barriers or mental blocks of lost concentration or poor timing in executing the technical elements of their programs.

What dream would you manifest if you knew you could not fail? Manifesting your dreams will require overcoming the limitations, boundaries and barriers of fear.

Chapter 3

SEEDS OF IDEAS

"There is one thing stronger than all the armies in the world and that is an idea whose time has come." – Victor Hugo

What are ideas? Why are they important? How do they relate to our dreams? Ideas are the seeds that stimulate our dreams to grow and flourish.

Our dreams begin in the form of seeds, which have the potential to become the things they are purposed to be. For example, a picture of an idea is not the actual thing but a design of what it could become. What ideas do you have for your dreams?

In order to write this book, I needed an idea for the title. Then, I began to think about ideas for the chapters in the form of an outline. The chapters are the structure, the bones to hold the book together. Each chapter requires substance to make the reading worthwhile. As ideas are sown, dream possibilities are grown. In order to multiply our ideas, we must put ourselves in an environment where others can stimulate them.

Ideas speak to our potential and possibilities. They say, "This is what I want to do and this is what I am capable of doing. This is what I believe I can do. I have the faith to accomplish this or that goal in life." The greater our faith level, the bigger our ideas become.

First, our ideas must have room to grow. We often limit our dreams when we choose an environment that is too small. It's like keeping a plant in its original pot and stifling its growth. Some plants will continue to outgrow the pot each time they are replanted. We must ask ourselves, "How big do I want my dream to become?" If we want to do great things, we must first believe that we were designed for greatness.

Secondly, we must know that there is greatness in our ideas. The seed itself has the potential to become the tree that bears fruit from other seeds within. The apple seed becomes the apple tree, which produces more apples that contain more seeds. One idea can become the catalyst that influences others to create innovative products and services.

Finally, great ideas put into action will produce great results through our dreams.

What separates a good idea from a great idea?

A good idea may be the answer to one problem but a great

SEEDS OF IDEAS   9 idea is one that multiplies and cannot be contained by its present environment. It's like an invention that sparks other inventions. It provides multiple solutions. A machine that only copies documents is a good idea. A multi-functional device that copies, scans and faxes documents is a great idea.

A phone that calls and retrieves messages is a good idea. A smartphone that has texting capabilities, internet capability, takes pictures and records videos is a great idea.

What ideas are you carrying that need to be acted upon? Take what you have and make it multiply.

Chapter 4

BEATING THE ODDS

"Do what you can, with what you have, where you are." –Theodore Roosevelt

Manifesting your dreams will require beating the odds. From our childhoods, some of us have faced unbeatable odds in the form of negative words spoken against our dreams.

"You'll never amount to anything."

"You ain't going to be nothing."

"Nothing good will become of your life."

Negativity is like poison injected into our bloodstream. If it is allowed to infiltrate our mind and thoughts, it will eventually influence our behavior. When we experience failures in life, our minds go back to those negative words and we start to believe that this is what was supposed to happen. "Death and life are in the power of the tongue: and they that love it shall eat the fruit thereof" (Proverbs 18:21). Odds seem overwhelming when we don't realize our true identity. We are born to succeed, designed for greatness and empowered to achieve.

To beat the odds, we must understand that every giant of doubt, unbelief and fear has an Achilles heel. The shepherd boy David defeated his giant, Goliath, by understanding his enemy. The bigger our giants, the greater the odds may seem stacked against us. A giant obstacle is in fact a giant opportunity for victory.

In card games, we speak of "bluffing." A bluff can be used to get your opponent to reveal the strength of the cards in their hand. Once you discover their strength, you can use your strength to defeat them. David bluffed Goliath with his appearance, the illusion that he was nothing but a weak and scrawny shepherd boy with a weapon that was obsolete compared to Goliath's armor, sword and shield. Goliath underestimated his opponent's secret weapon, which was the name of the Lord. The God of Battles was in the battle with David to assure him victory over Goliath. Regardless of the odds against your dreams, God and you have the upper hand.

In the betting arena, bigger odds result in a larger payoff. In our quest to manifest our dreams, we receive greater strength, greater faith and greater confidence to do greater things. Part of beating the odds requires that we remind ourselves of the things we've already accomplished. David defeated the lion and the bear, which gave him the confidence and faith to fight against Goliath.

I've survived a job layoff, a business loss and a $10k decrease in salary, and I know the odds are in my favor to advance my dreams to become financially independent and fulfilled with my career. There's a dreamer in every survivor. Beating the odds is all about survival, even if it sometimes requires working with less to accomplish more.

Chapter 5

SURVIVING DREAM STORMS

"Storm survivors are equipped for great success."

What are dream storms? How do they threaten your success? How do you weather them?

Storms don't come to last; they come to pass. Dream storms form from elements that threaten the life of your dreams. One type of dream storm is a recession or economic collapse. You may find yourself unemployed, underemployed or without any income. This type of storm gives you feelings of despair and hopelessness and leaves you with the thoughts that you can no longer pursue your dreams. It's like an earthquake that shakes your world from its very foundation.

I believe our dreams are built on hope for change and a better future. We hope that our futures are bigger, better and brighter when we move in the direction of our dreams. A dream storm is designed to leave you busted and disgusted. We tend to focus on the lost job, lost finances, car or home. You may have lost a job but you did not lose your skills and talents. Your creative ideas are your transportation to your next station in life and your home is the environment that you carry in your heart. A storm may disrupt your home but it cannot take away your choice to live with peace in your mind. The storm may affect what happens to you, but you can control what happens *in you*. You can weather any storm if you chose to go through it, grow through it and change your perspective.

Other storms may destroy material things but they cannot take away the things that make us storm survivors. I remember the accident that totaled my Toyota Tercel. I was so thankful that the car was the only thing that was destroyed. I did not fret over the lost vehicle. Instead, I got out of the car in a state of calmness and total peace. This storm may have destroyed a possession but it made me stronger in dealing with adversity, discomfort and handling difficult situations. My "old" dream car was lost but after the storm, I was able to upgrade to a nicer model. The same storm that's designed to take out your dreams, can also work to elevate you to the next level of dream manifestation.

Another dream storm is like an earthquake I suffered during my Georgia Tech years when I was pursuing a degree in Industrial Engineering. One quarter, I went on academic probation due to poor grades. This storm came to test my perseverance, determination and endurance. How would I adapt to this situation and become a survivor of my dream, as opposed to becoming a college dropout? I remember obtaining academic counseling and making changes to my study habits. This was a time of tremendous growth and maturation for me. It was time to pick up the pieces and step up to a greater commitment in learning. I learned that adaptability is the key to survival and that we must look for the light at the end of the tunnel as we walk in the direction of our dreams.

It's also quite prophetic and ironic that I lived near a tunnel. Whenever I walked through the tunnel, it was dark inside but as I continued to walk, I could see the light, which led me out of the tunnel. Storms are like tunnels: They're dark when you're in them, but as you weather them they dissipate and reveal the light.

Chapter 6

DREAM ANCHORS

"Imagine yourself so inspired that you find yourself perspiring with relentless determination."

When we encounter dream storms in the form of boisterous waves and billowing winds, we must anchor our dreams to prevent our dreams from being shipwrecked and lost at sea. The four anchors that hold our dreams intact during these storms are **imagination, inspiration, perspiration** and **determination.**

We've all heard that knowledge is power. Imagination is greater than knowledge because it removes limitations and constraints and speaks to our potential and the possibilities within our ideas. Knowledge alone will confine us to doing things the way we've always done them, but imagination enables us to think outside of the box and attempt something different. I may know how to cook a meal one way, but if I imagine doing something different with the ingredients, I can create a dish that has never been tasted before.

When you find yourself in a rut with your dreams, imagination will give you a fresh start and show you how to rise above your circumstances. I remember during high school pep rallies we would march in the gym and make a crisscross or "X" formation in the center of the basketball court. I suggested that we could march along a "U" formation on the floor instead. We tried it, and everyone loved the new formation.

The next anchor is inspiration. Inspiration is like a breath of fresh air. Oxygen is necessary for our survival in the natural world, and inspiration is the oxygen that gives life to our dreams.

Not only do we need air, we need fresh air. What's in the air that you are breathing? What's inspiring your ideas? When I'm on a cruise vacation in the open ocean away from traffic, air pollution, toxic factories and burning contaminants, the air is cleaner, fresher, and easier to breathe. Inspiration comes through our natural environment. So many negative elements oppose our dreams that we must find shelter to be inspired to start, continue, and manifest our dreams. Inspiration gives strength to keep trying when dream storms blow. Inspiration is the place of soliloquy in the midst of a hurricane. It keeps our dreams intact when everything is falling apart around us.

Inspiration is like fuel to a car. It's vital for starting the car and keeping it running. There are different grades of fuel such as regular, mid-grade and premium. Depending on our journey and season in life, we may require premium grade inspiration especially if the storm is long-lived. Inspiration not only speaks to us daily but it speaks to our season. It gives us sustaining power to pursue our dreams and hold fast to them until the dream storm passes over.

How do we receive inspiration? It may be a word written or spoken by another. It may be a new thought or idea that comes to our mind. It may be a scene of beauty in nature. It may be something experienced through our five senses. Classical music inspires me. Motivational speakers and books inspire me. A movie such as "The Great Debaters" or "Akeelah and the Bees" that depicts someone triumphing over overwhelming circumstances inspires me. We must find our source of inspiration and tap into it so that we have the fuel that's needed to manifest our dreams. Inspiration is all around us if we only recognize it and inhale deeply.

After inspiration, we need to employ the anchor of perspiration. I always tell people who go to the fitness center, "If you can feel it, that means it's working." Pain produces results. It's resistance to the weights that produces the strength of the muscles. Strong storms produce strong survivors. The greater the obstacles overcome, the greater your dreams become.

What makes you perspire? All busy work is not necessarily productivity. There is nothing worse than spinning our wheels and going nowhere. We must know where to focus our efforts if we are to manifest our dreams during stormy seasons. We must know what to study if we are to make the best possible grade

DREAM ANCHORS   19 on a test. Perspiration is about sacrifice. It's giving up a present comfort or pleasure for a future success or accomplishment. When we choose to commit to fitness and a healthy diet in the present, we can realize a more attractive and healthier body, in the future.

Some storms can cut off our resources and we must learn to live on the reserves. We must take less and do more with it. Having less time and money may require expending more energy and perspiration to achieve the same results. One of my enjoyments in life is working on the lawn. I find it quite therapeutic and relaxing to cultivate plants and landscape the yard, which causes perspiration. When I see the finished product of a well-manicured lawn and the blooming flowers I have planted, I can stand back and say the finished product was worth the effort.

Let's recap the first three dream anchors: Imagination provides a fresh start. Inspiration gives sustaining power to keep going. Perspiration produces results. The fourth anchor is determination which speaks of our intestinal fortitude, indomitable will, or grit that compels us to stick with a thing until we receive the expected results.

Anyone who is naturally competitive will engage in a sport, game, or event until they can find a way to win. We must hold fast to our dreams and not relinquish the helm when storm winds blow and bring adverse conditions our way. What's the use of running if you don't cross the finish line? What's the use of beginning a project, if you don't see it until completion? What's the use of dreaming if you do not experience dream manifestation?

Determination begins with a made-up mind. It's like the Little Engine That Could. As it climbed the hill, it began saying, "I think I can, I think I can." As it continued along the way, it changed its mantra to, "I know I can, I know I can." How we think and behave ultimately determines our outcome. For the survivor of dream storms, quitting is not an option. What things in life are you determined to do, become, and have?

Chapter 7

OLYMPIC DREAM MOMENTS

The best athlete does not always finish first. In the Olympics, the gold medal winner must complete one event or a series of events to outperform their competition. He or she may hold the world record for this event, or even be the reigning World Champion but if they cannot beat their competition, they will find themselves in second or third place or with no medal at all.

Some dreams must be manifested in a specific moment in time. The moment of a lifetime is in the lifetime of the moment. All the training, competitions and conditioning have prepared the athlete for this one moment in time. In order to realize our Olympic dream moment, we must prepare for it, recognize it and seize it. To be successful, we must prepare for opportunities.

I believe that practice improves performance and enables us to execute with confidence and ease. However, the way we handle an event during the "big moment" is greatly influenced by our mental toughness. Recognizing our dream moment requires a discernment of our times and seasons and knowing what to do. The time to be ready is not the time to get ready. Any Olympian who is selected for the Olympics team has already met the qualifications through their preparation and performance. The real question that must be answered is what they will do during the moment that counts.

Fear is not an option. Failure is not an option. To win the gold medal, you must be able to execute with precision and outperform, outplay, and out class the rest of the competition. You must be able to compete against yourself and defeat the enemies within. Doubt must exit your mind. Unbelief must leave your thinking. Every excuse for not being your best must be replaced by words like, "This is my moment, this is my time and this is my season to seize the moment. I am engineered for greatness. I am designed for excellence. I am destined to win."

What Olympic dream moment are you preparing for? How are you preparing for this moment?

What obstacles do you need to overcome to realize this moment?

Part of competing is being able to deal with disappointment. All athletes compete to win, but only the ones with the best results will take the podium. What should we do when we fall short of our winning expectations? First, we must understand that we are not failures. We only failed to meet our expectations in the competition. A loss can be very disappointing especially when others also had high expectations for us to win. The best that we can expect from ourselves is to do the best we can under the circumstances.

After the event, we can think of a plethora of things that we could have done differently: a quicker start, a faster pace, a stronger finish. Did I execute with confidence, precision, and control? Did I underestimate the abilities of my competition? Why didn't I seize the moment?

I know from experience that mental toughness can make or break a competition regardless of skill level or expertise. In 2013, I was competing at an area-level international speech contest. After two minutes of speaking, the timekeeper turned on the green light early. I totally lost my focus of where I should be in the speech. If the light was correct, I only had two minutes to complete the speech, I had only gotten to the introduction and the first speaking point. I tried to make eye contact with the timekeeper to confirm that a timing mistake had occurred, but to no avail. After a long, noticeable pause, the damage had been done and was irreparable. I would liken it to a false start in track and field, only I had started on time but became lost because the timing signal gave a false reading. I had a great topic, but under the circumstances the speech was a fiasco.

Looking back, I began to ask myself what I could have done differently in retrospect. One thought was to openly address the timekeeper's mistake and ask for the opportunity to begin again. The only thing about this course of action was that it would have appeared to the audience that the mistake was mine, since no one else could see the timing device except for the two timekeepers and me. Would the timekeeper have had the integrity to admit his mistake?

Another thought was to stage a protest with the contest master. Later, I looked in the rule book; it appears the rules do not cover this scenario, so she probably would not have known what to do in this situation. How can you protest the outcome if the rules do not address the reason for your protest?

In all competitions, we can learn from our mistakes, and the one thing I learned was the importance of dealing with distractions. A loss of focus for even a few seconds can make or break your ability to execute. The take-away from this experience is to never allow a distraction to impede your mental toughness. We cannot control what happens to us but we can control what happens *in us*.

This experience was a disappointing moment for me, but I decided not to let it define my destiny. It became the launching pad for this book, which I titled "Manifesting Your Dreams." This moment of disappointment became my experience, and I decided to move out of disappointment by shifting gears and moving into making a comeback from this loss. Several years ago, I read a book by motivational speaker Willie Jolley called "A Setback is a Setup for a Comeback." This experience was the setup for my comeback.

In manifesting our dreams, we must be able to turn lemons into lemonade, bitterness into sweetness, defeats into victories, and disappointments into comebacks. A loss opportunity is a gained experience to use for future triumphs. Think of it as investment into your mental toughness bank account that will produce dividends in your dream portfolio.

I like the words of the Apostle Paul that say he was persecuted but not forsaken, cast down but not destroyed (2 Cor. 4:9). For those who don't know, this guy was beaten with rods, stoned and shipwrecked three times (2 Cor. 11:25). He was able to say, "Forgetting those things which are behind, and reaching forth to those things which are before" (Phil 3:13).

We must understand that sometimes a disappointment is simply a divine delay for something greater to come in our future. Think of it as a stepping-stone, launching pad, springboard, or simply the setup for the comeback. The destined appointment follows the disappointment if we learn from the experience and move towards the future opportunity.

Chapter 8

LIVE YOUR DREAMS

"The only person you are destined to become is the person you decide to be." –Ralph Waldo Emerson

What does it mean to live your dreams? It's one thing to read and talk about the dreams of others. This was what someone else did with his or her life. Their life story may be inspiring, but this is not your dream. We can learn from their experiences and often find a connection with their plight or struggle. The thing we should not do is live our lives through the dreams of others.

Often, children are stifled in their dreams by trying to live the dreams of their parents. Dreams our parents wanted for themselves or failed to pursue are passed down to children. It is imperative that parents discern the abilities and talents of their children and guide them in those directions. If your child is a musician, don't force them to become an athlete. Help them discover their passions in life in order to live their dreams.

I have always been an avid learner and focused on academics, so it's no coincidence that I have a passion for teaching in whatever I do. I have a knack for making learning simpler for those who are struggling academically. One of my challenges was tutoring my nephew, Christian in Latin, which was not a language I had previously studied. I was able to use my understanding of French and apply it to teaching Latin. As a result, Christian raised his grade by a letter. Even when we find ourselves in uncharted waters, our gifts will enable us to do things we may not have experience doing. The principles of learning are proven and tested. When we exercise our gifts, we are living our dreams and we do what we were designed to do.

Living your dreams is living in the present as you prepare for the future. Some dreams are seasonal and must be done in the right season of your life. At forty years old, your dream of becoming a professional basketball player is probably a pipe dream, especially if you have never played on a professional level. I may have played tennis throughout high school, college and competed in ALTA tennis post-graduation, but at fifty-five years of age my season to play professionally is over. Living your dreams is not trying to relive your past.

Our dreams may be a part of the legacy left by another dreamer. MLK's dream spoke to the consciousness of a nation. His legacy has paved the way for many of us to live our dreams.

We have a right to live our dreams. Our dreams are embedded in the rights to life, liberty and the pursuit of happiness. As we exercise our rights to vote, speak freely, and practice our religious beliefs, we have the right to live our dreams. What's preventing you from living your dreams?

LIVE YOUR DREAMS

Chapter 9

DREAM FIGHTERS

With every dream, there are opposing forces in nature that do not want to see your dream manifested.

In this corner, weighing in at 6 lbs. 3 ounces is Baby Dreamer. In the other corner, weighing in at 160 lbs. is the dream opponent. At the sound of the bell, come out fighting.

The dream is birthed inside of the dreamer. The cries become syllables, the syllables become words, the words become sentences, and the sentences become paragraphs that describe, articulate and prophesy the dream. Words like, "When I grow up, I'm going to help people learn how to tap into their potential, discover their greatness and manifest their dreams." The opposition punches back with words like, "You can't do this because you are not good enough and will never amount to anything." The fight is on, the battle rages, and the war is unending in the struggle to liberate our dreams.

Moses had a dream to see the Israelites freed from Egyptian slavery. He spoke truth to power and told King Pharaoh, "Let my people go." This freedom was not offered the first time Moses made his request. There was a conflict between opposing forces, which led to numerous trips to the King's palace. The performance of miracles and twelve plagues later, Pharaoh finally yielded to Moses' request. Moses kept asking, seeking and knocking, and the doorway to his dream finally opened.

The Israelites encountered a final battle at the Red Sea as they were pursued by Pharaoh's armies. When all looked lost and the dream of escape appeared to be over for them, God showed up and fought their battle. The fight was fixed for them because all they had to do was hold their peace and let God fight their battle. The battle is not entirely yours, but it belongs to the God of dream fighters. Sometimes, all we have to do is show up and God will show out for us. The reality of our dreams is the dream in our realities. The real thing about dreams is that we actually dream about things that are real.

In tenth grade, I played the trumpet in the high school band at Northside. That year, it was my lot to wear braces, which impaired my ability to play. I was instructed to wear wax over the braces so they would not cut into my mouth as I played. My band instructor gave me a "B" in the class because he felt my playing abilities were not good enough. Band was one of my favorite classes. I had made an "A" in band my freshman year and I made a decision to fight for my grade point average. My dream that year was to make "all A's" and this included band.

To make a long story short, I went to my instructor and he required me to play the selection from our band festival. I was not a novice to music. I began my music career in fifth grade, singing in chorus and learning to play the recorder. By this time, I knew how to sight-read as well as play by ear. I showed up and played the selection, but it was God who gave me the skill to play with precision and accuracy in spite of the braces. The same prophetic breath that spoke dreams concerning my life now played notes that manifested the dream. In a dream fight, we must know who we are, what we have and what we can do. I was a skilled musician, I had God-given talent, and I knew how to read music and play by ear. I learned the importance of fighting for my dreams.

Dreaming is a right, but manifesting your dreams requires a fight. If our dreams are worth living for, they certainly must also be worth fighting for. In 2007, I stood in line for about five hours to exercise my right to vote. I had strong convictions about doing this because I knew that someone had given their life so that I could have this right. Only when we stand for our dreams, will others be able to stand on our shoulders and fight for their dreams. When we fight for our rights and win, we have a greater appreciation for the things that we fought for. It gives value, substance, significance, and meaning to our dreams. We cherish the moment.

Proverbs 13:19 says it this way: "The desire accomplished is sweet to the soul." Julius Caesar said, "Veni, vidi, vici," which means "I came, I saw, I conquered."

Chapter 10

DREAM YOUR WAY OUT!

Are you working a dead-end job and finding yourself in a rut? Do you know there is more in life for you to do but simply can't find a way to fulfill your calling? We must understand that corporate America does not promote our dreams unless they can control our ideas and make a profit from our innovations. At a one-on-one session with my former manager, I explained to him that what I desire to do is bigger than what this company would allow me to do. When we see and speak through the eyes and voice of a dreamer, it gives us a way out of the most abysmal and bleakest situations. In corporate America, we experience the "glass ceiling" syndrome, but the hammer that shatters this ceiling is the manifestation of our dreams.

After working 15 years at AT&T, I had climbed the corporate ladder to the ranks of Project Specialist. I was making plans to advance in the ranks during the next five years, and then the unexpected happened. The company downsized and I was given sixty days to find another job with the company or leave the payroll. I did receive a severance package, which allowed me to stay afloat until I could find another job. The glass ceiling suddenly became the glass floor because I had to start over again from the bottom of the ladder.

I was unemployed for about a year before I began with a temporary agency. Most prospective employers said I was overqualified for the positions that I was pursuing. After a year of temp work for Coca-Cola, I sought permanent employment with them. In the end, they would not hire me permanently, so I knew it was time to find another company where I could become permanent. I have learned that permanent employment is only a temporary solution if you are destined to do greater things in life. In corporate America, we must constantly upgrade our skills or end up in a stuck place and become obsolete. The longer we stay with a company, the harder it is to dream our way out. We become complacent in an environment of people who believe that what they have now is the best that it is and will ever be for them. Dreaming our way out requires that we reject complacency, the status quo and anything that would hold us down or keep us from moving forward with our aspirations.

Dreaming our way out leads to the time of awakening when we see ourselves in the future and things look bigger, better and brighter. We must make the best of bad situations, but we really have to use our imaginations. The brain is designed to solve problems, so we must think our way out of our present situation.

If we are to enter into our land of dream manifestation, we must shatter the glass ceiling mentality and think outside the box. After working for these kinds of companies for over twenty-five years, it's time to create my own company and embrace my destiny. The dreamer envisions the CEO in YOU. You are the brand, the product, the service, the tag and the label. When your clients buy into you, they must know how they will benefit.

Chapter 11

DREAM CONTENDERS VS. DREAM PRETENDERS

Is your dream the real thing or simply a "knock off" version of the genuine article? Can you reproduce your results with consistency and authenticity? In championship games and tournaments, the contenders are separated from the pretenders as the event progresses to the next round. Pretenders may produce a fluke upset along the way, but a true contender can reproduce their winning results. If you have the goods, you must know it and show it. It has been said that experience is the best teacher, and if we have learned from our past mistakes in life we can use this knowledge to our advantage.

Fate or destiny will sometimes give us a second chance to prove ourselves in manifesting our dreams.

In her third Grand Slam Final at the 2014 Australian Open, Li Na finally won the championship. For her, the third time was the charm. In order to have a third shot at the title, Na had to reproduce her winning results in defeating the pretenders and contenders. Pretenders can simply show up and play, whereas contenders must show up and display the goods. A pretender can execute with tentativeness and fear, but a contender must execute with precision and courage. Pretenders can bluff their opponents and hope to topple them, whereas contenders know their opponents and exploit their weakness in defeating them.

Dream Contenders are made of tough stuff. Their ideas are solid, their plans are concrete, and their impact is life-changing. Contenders begin with a solid dream foundation. The dream is based on reality and not a fantasy. The dream is at the right place and the right time.

Doing the right thing in the right place at the right time makes the difference between seized or missed opportunities. The man or woman contending for political office is prepared before the office becomes vacant. The pretender is play-acting with a "fake it until I make it" attitude. A solid dream foundation will weather dream storms and stand the test of time.

Next, the true dream contender has a plan or strategy for execution. They have written down their vision, set realistic goals and are moving in the direction of their dreams. Contenders know how to count the cost in terms of what it will take to manifest their dreams. This could be their strategic plan. The thought process is, "This is where I would like to be, and this is what it will take for me to get there."

To win the championship or title, a contender must have a strategy for defeating their opponent. If my backhand is strong, I must find a way to capitalize on it, using it to my advantage by hitting to my opponent's weaker side. If my opponent has a weak backhand volley, I must exploit this weakness by serving and hitting to their backhand. Part of my preparation strategy could include practicing to make two out of every three serves to the backhand of my opponent. To win, I must be able to execute consistently.

Finally, a contender's results are felt in a tangible way. Are you inspired to do something differently? Have you changed your way of thinking about your current situation? Do you see things differently as a result of a new perspective? One thing we learned from Li Na is that you should never give up on your dream in spite of your age or past defeats. At age 31, she became the first Asian player to win the Australian Open. Her impact on other players would be to not allow age or nationality to be a determining factor in contending for their dreams.

Chapter 12

DREAM PEARLS

What's in your treasure of dreams? Dream pearls? Dream diamonds? Opportunities of gold?

We all have valuable treasures locked deep within our hearts and minds. According to 2 Corinthians 4:7, "But we have this treasure in earthen vessels, that the excellency of the power may be of God and not of us." The challenge is to bring it to the surface and polish it up and create something beautiful with it. This process involves mining, refining, and designing our dream treasures. Each of us is an original masterpiece with original thoughts and ideas. We have the potential for greatness locked inside our dream treasures.

A dream must go through the process of irritation. Consider the pearl, which is formed when a foreign object like a grain of sand is introduced into a mussel or oyster. The animal coats the irritant with a substance called *nacre*, the material with which it builds its shell. Layers of *nacre* build up to form a pearl. Likewise, our dreams are a byproduct of things that "rock our world" and irritate our environment. A broken marriage cultivates within us the desire to find more meaningful relationships or live life to the fullest as a single. A loss or dead-end job sends us on the quest to explore new career opportunities, find a better job or even launch our own business. The irritant is the catalyst for the formation of the dream pearl.

After, pearls are formed, they must be harvested and drilled and matched for stringing. This describes the mining and designing phases of our dream pearls. The pearl harvesting season is in the winter months because the oyster's metabolism is slowed and *nacre* deposits result in better luster on the pearl. We must harvest our dream pearls during our season of brilliance. This is the time that we are radiating ideas and creativity. I believe that when we slow down our metabolism through quiet meditation and reflection we experience an increase in innovative brilliance.

The designing process in manufacturing pearls involves sorting, drilling and stringing. First, similar looking pearls are blended together so they appear to match. The analogy is that our skill sets work together in creating our dream pearls. Understanding my gift at teaching, motivates me to teach as a public speaker and also teach as a writer. The next stage is drilling the hole through the pearl, which must be done with precision and accuracy. A talent or gift that is misaligned can do more damage than good to the one receiving it. The ways our gifts are aligned affect the way we display them. The final stage is stringing and blending, which requires culling through about 10,000 pearls to find enough to assemble together to make a single necklace. In life, we enter and exit a large number of relationships. Everyone cannot be on your string of dream pearls because they do not blend with your destiny. A winning team must have the right chemistry in order to become all they are designed to be. Dream teams have dream pearls meticulously placed on the same string.

Chapter 13

DREAM DIAMONDS

Similar to pearls, diamonds also must go through the process of mining, refining and designing. Diamond is formed in huge pressure and heat, deep within the Earth. They are brought close to the Earth's surface through deep volcanic eruptions by magma, which cools into igneous rocks known as kimberlites and lamproites. How does this compare to dream diamonds? We are often forced to go after our dreams when the pressure to remain the same is greater than the pressure to change. If you're doing the same thing over and over again and not making any noticeable change or measurable progress, it's time to pursue your dream diamonds.

Circumstances and situations in life can not only place pressure on our lives, but they can also cause us to feel the heat of bills, lost possessions, lost relationships and lost years. One major storm can rock your world. When we are given deadlines to make a mortgage payment and the funds are not there, we find ourselves in the hot seat. We must search our options to find the money. Do I borrow it from someone else? Do I take it from my retirement? When the funds are available, we don't have to sweat the small stuff, but when they are not we must find a way to come up with the money. In this search for resources, we often discover our dream diamonds being formed in the heat of our circumstances. Bam! I have an idea for making money.

First the pressure, then the heat, and now the volcanic eruption that brings the diamonds to the surface. If things get uncomfortable enough, you will make a move. When you get sick and tired of being sick and tired, you will do something about your present plight. It's like the fight-or-flight syndrome. When we are placed in harm's way, our adrenaline kicks in and we go into survival mode. We decide to swim and not sink, run and not stand still, fight and not be defeated. We activate our dream diamonds and undergo the refining process.

Rough diamonds are taken to major cutting centers in Israel, Antwerp, Bombay, Johannesburg and New York, where they are marked and usually sawed. Our dream diamonds must also be cut so they can be polished and cleaned before they are placed on display for sale. Many of us begin with raw talents and skills, which must be trained and developed so that we can become the best. We must cut away bad habits and ineffective ways of doing things. For example, a singer who is trained in vocal techniques performs with ease by breathing properly which adds value and quality to her singing ability. When we train to use our gifts properly, we get better use from them and they will add longevity to our performance.

One of the greatest compliments that we can receive is that we were polished and professional. I believe everyone who understands the value of their dream diamonds wants them to look great and sparkle with brilliance when they are placed on display.

Chapter 14

OPPORTUNITIES OF GOLD

Some would call them "golden opportunities." It's all about being prepared for these opportunities of gold to cash in and seize the moment.

One way to refine gold is to heat it in a crucible. Stirring causes the impurities, or *dross,* to rise to the top of the molten metal so they can be skimmed off. Our lives go through a similar refining process to reveal our true nature or character. Before we can seize these opportunities of gold, our fears, doubts and lack of belief in our talents and ourselves must be purified away. Tests and trials come to make us stronger, not weaker. They make us stable, not insecure.

As we go through the fires of refinement, we grow. Though talent can take us to the top of our field, it takes character to sustain us. There are no shortcuts to character development.

In this quest for gold, we must deal with failure, defeat, disappointment, and rejection. Each failure refines us for future successes. Each defeat toughens us up for future victories. Each disappointment sets us up for divine appointments. Every rejection molds us into a sought-out commodity.

Once the vessel has been refined, it can carry its weight in gold and has the capacity to perform up to the gold standard of its given task. In preparing for a competition, an Olympian must undergo many hours of practice each day to win an event lasting only a few short moments. Two-time Olympic gold medalist Shani Davis says he prepares 4 to 6 hours a day for an event lasting about two minutes.

Opportunities of gold must be recognized and pursued, and deep digging is required to manifest them. There are two types of opportunities: ones we prepare for and ones we create. The opportunity of the moment is in the moment of the opportunity. If you don't recognize it, you can't pursue it. If you are not prepared, you cannot manifest it.

Back in 1999, a position became available with AT&T for a Technical Consultant. I had been in my current position for several years and I decided to pursue this opportunity. The hiring manager asked me why I wanted to be selected for the position. I explained to her my credentials, which included completing a program for several weeks to prepare for management. She was impressed with my preparation and I was able to seize this opportunity of gold.

Opportunities of gold may be all around us, but they will do

46   MANIFESTING YOUR DREAMS

us no good if we cannot find them and tap into them. Gold miners call it *prospecting*. A prospect is an opportunity for something to happen. This is the potential, possibility, or probability to discover gold. Prospects may be found in the dreams flowing underneath our river of ideas. The key is to tap into that stream and bring it to the surface. If we don't act on our ideas, someone else will.

One idea I had back in the early '80s was for a pen and pencil cushion. I had the material for the product but did not take advantage of this opportunity of gold. Needless to say, someone else had the same idea, and today I purchase their products rather than having them buy my products.

Chapter 15

DREAM MERCHANTS

How valuable is your dream? Before others can recognize its true value, it must first have value to you. The things that we value in life, we take care of them. If you value your health, you will place a high priority on your diet, your fitness level and obtaining the proper amount of sleep or rest. Likewise, are you feeding your dreams the proper nutrients to make them manifest? When was the last time you got on the treadmill and exercised your dreams? Are you resting enough to have the awakening energy to cultivate your dream landscape, or "dreamscape"?

Consumers purchasing a product tend to examine it for its quality to see how long it will last. Quality reflects the amount of thought and time placed into developing it. If we value our money, we value the things we buy with our money. I have owned three Toyota Camrys because they are reliable. Some may consider the Camry a cheap car, but there are some expensive cars with high maintenance records and poor performance levels on the road.

Dream merchants know how to sell ideas, experiences, winning strategies and success stories. They show people how to live better lives by getting more out of life. The value in each day is the gift it brings to take another chance, try again and seize another dream moment.

What you get out of life is directly related to what you put into life. Quality input results in quality output. Valuable input results in valuable output. There are no shortcuts to creating a product that will stand the test of time. We must grow through the process that defines our destiny.

Is your dream built to last or will it just become another fad that's here today and gone tomorrow? Will there always be a need for the product that you have to offer? If I purchase your product, how will it benefit my life or impact the lives of others? If it changes the way we think, it will benefit our actions.

Before you can change your diet, you must change the way you think about food. If you are eating for nutritional value, you will make wiser choices in the foods that you eat. Those who eat for immediate gratification will go after junk food and fast food in a heartbeat. You must ask yourself, what's fueling your dreams? Am I going after fame, fortune, prestige, etc., or do I want to change the world?

DREAM MERCHANTS   49

A dream merchant sells a vision and a mission. If you buy into the dream, it will enable you to do, become, achieve, accomplish and manifest your dreams. Dream merchants are agents of change who challenge you to expand your vision and live with a mission.

A Japanese proverb says, "Vision without action is a daydream; action without vision is a nightmare." In order to get the best use of this product, you must take action. It's like buying exercise equipment and never using it. The product that's designed to make you look and feel better does you no good if it's left in the box or placed in a corner to gather dust. The real value in the product of a dream merchant is its motivation for you to take action.

Exercise your dream and it will beat you into shape by challenging you, transforming you, and stretching you. If you can feel its effects, then you know that it's working.

Three years ago, I began a membership with Planet Fitness. What inspired me to join was a cruise I had taken the previous year. After about three days of exercise in the fitness center, I could feel results. The revelation for me was that I needed to keep doing this on a regular basis. Once you realize the potential and potency in the product, you will buy into it to continue reaping the benefits. Exercising your dream increases your energy level in life. You'll look forward to getting up each day and feel a greater sense of self-worth through your achievements. You are fortified with your daily dose of dream vitamins, minerals, and supplements for life.

There's a psychology to selling, in that the thoughts that we associate with actions give the results we expect to achieve. For example, if you have a cold and take chicken soup and drink orange juice, you will feel better. The key is to boost your immune system so it can fight off the attack and return the body to good health. Dream merchants know that people invest in products which they expect to yield results.

Rest is a highly effective habit for the dream merchant. The body must have down time to recover. You can't eat all the time without resting your digestive system. Neither can you exercise all the time without resting your muscles and other organs and systems that enable the body to function normally.

The product you must have is the one that you can't do without. You think about it subconsciously when you're sleeping because you've carried it throughout the day. Time spent in rest and repose prepares you for the next dream workout. You're ready for greater resistance, greater challenges, and greater opportunities to fortify your dream. You can't stay in your comfort zone any longer. It's time to up the ante and increase the size of weights, number of repetitions and length of practice. Resting tends to renew your strength. It refreshes your mind and restores your soul.

Dream merchants believe in their products and know that they will work if you use them. The power of knowledge is not in the knowledge itself, but the use of the knowledge. When potential or stored energy is turned into kinetic energy or motion, impact takes place. There is power in the product.

Warning: This dream innovation is non-hazardous to your health because it will revolutionize your life! Let the buyer beware.

DREAM MERCHANTS

Chapter 16

DREAM BUILDERS

Faith, hope, endurance and perseverance are the pillars we base our dreams upon. Dreams are built on invisible things that manifest into visible things. Before we can realize them in our present reality, we must see them through the eyes of faith. Hebrews 11:1 says, "Now faith is the substance of things hoped for, the evidence of things not seen." The things that we achieve in life begin with our belief system.

May 5th, 2014 marked the high school graduation of my niece. Those that dream of graduating realize they must do the things necessary to make that future dream a present reality. A dream of this magnitude requires at least four years of commitment to academic pursuits through much discipline and hard work. It's similar to the game of baseball. If we are to make it to home plate, we must begin with the goal in mind and touch each base

52

until we make it to home base. Some players reach home standing up whereas others slide home in a more dramatic fashion. There are different ways to get home but everyone who makes it started with the end in mind and continued through their journey until their goal was achieved.

Faith, the first pillar, can be described as a powerful substance that produces tangible results when acted upon. Faith is a walk, an action, and a journey. The dreams we manifest in life are rooted and grounded in our ability to move toward them and make them happen even when we don't feel like moving forward. Exercising faith requires movement and movement changes our emotions.

Faith is a lifestyle for those who believe in the power of their dreams. Many times in life, we must ask ourselves why we began our journey towards our destination, and then return to our faith, which says, "Because I believed I could do it."

Our faith speaks of our expectations for the future. The achievements we accomplish in life are a direct result of our level of faith. Faith the size of a mustard seed can move mountains, according to Matthew 17:20. The dreams I have achieved in my life were built upon my faith to manifest them. Faith finds a way to attract the necessary resources to build our dreams. Faith is the foundation we walk on when we don't see the way to go. It's similar to the scene in the movie, "Indiana Jones and the Last Crusade." Indy had to walk across a ravine but saw nothing to get him across. As he stepped out into the air, the bridge to support him miraculously appeared beneath his feet. As we walk in the direction of our dreams, the unseen forces in

DREAM BUILDERS   53 nature are attracted to us in support of our dreams. Our role is to take the first step, start walking, and keep walking until we reach our destination.

The second pillar is hope, which is our expectation in the dream. It is the pillar that keeps the dream alive in our hearts. Reverend Jesse Jackson coined the phrase "keep hope alive." As long as we have hope, we will keep moving forward. Hope is patiently waiting on the promise to be fulfilled. Our hope sustains us in the present and speaks to our future by telling us something better is on the way if we stay the course and keep moving in faith. Hope keeps the promise within our reach. A hopeless dream is doomed to fail but a hopeful dream is destined to succeed.

We all have hope for things like graduation, career advancement, successful marriage, material possessions, etc. If we are to manifest our dreams, we cannot lose hope in them. God's plan for us is to give us a hope and a future, according to Jeremiah 29:11. We must hope in our future and have a future in our hope. We must hope in our possibilities and have possibilities in our hope. We must hope in our dreams and have dreams in our hope. Our heart becomes sick when hope is deferred, but accomplishing our desires is sweet to the soul, according to Proverbs 13:12&19. In our journey to manifestation, we must not lose hope but take it to the limits of our faith and receive the promise of our dreams. We must take hope to the limit one more time.

The third pillar is endurance because endurance is more important than speed or strength in completing a race. Many people are great starters but lousy finishers. Think about the number of projects that we begin and give up on before they are completed. Often, we stop believing and hoping in our ability to manifest our dreams. We run out of energy and just give up.

My journey towards college graduation was one of endurance. I took the long, scenic route to get out. Over the course of eight years and three changes of major, I was able to earn my diploma on March 13th, 1987. I learned that endurance is required to adapt to your surroundings and adaptation is the key to survival. There were many setbacks, disappointing moments and disheartening grades, but the strength to endure did not come without a price.

Endurance is like testing yourself to see how fast you can run or how heavy a weight you can lift. It reveals the amount of stress and pressure you can withstand. It prepares you for the next test. The longer I can withstand the present challenge, the more stamina I have to withstand the next one. I like the definition in Webster's dictionary, which is "power to last and to withstand hard wear." Endurance is the power that conditions us with the strength to manifest our dreams.

The fourth pillar is perseverance, or not giving up on what we have set out to do. It speaks to our will to succeed at our dreams. Perseverance tells us to keep going when we feel like quitting. We must continue in a race if we are to cross the finish line.

Perseverance and endurance can be thought of as twins. Endurance is the means, and perseverance is the ends.

DREAM BUILDERS

Perseverance causes us to endure and endurance enables us to persevere. Let's return back to our baseball analogy: I may have the perseverance to run from first base to home plate, but I must also have the endurance to make it from home to first, first to second, second to third, and third base to home plate. A lack of perseverance will inhibit our ability to endure, and a lack of endurance will disable our perseverance. Perseverance says, "You have to want to manifest your dreams." If we are willing to persevere with obedience to endure, we shall reap the reward of dream manifestation.

Dream builders walk on the foundation of their faith, stand in hope for the promise of their dreams, undergo endurance training for conditioning and employ perseverance to complete the assignment.

Chapter 17

Exercising Dream Options

Everyone wants to look good physically but few are willing to invest the time and effort that it takes to obtain and maintain a well-defined body. We see people in the media who we desire and aspire to be like and often dream of how we would look if we had their physiques. A good-looking body goes a long way to building our self-confidence and receiving comments from others when we go out in public. We feel a sense of accomplishment when we feel and see definition added to our muscles and weight loss when we step on the scales.

A dream does not take proper shape or form by standing still. We must decide on its appearance and then do whatever it takes to work it into shape. Cardiovascular training is the heart of the dream workout. Running faster increases our heart rate and gets the adrenaline flowing. Sprints are easy distances to run, but manifesting our dreams is more like running a marathon. Back at Northside High, when I ran track in tenth grade, I loved to run the 100-yard and 220-yard dashes, but I hated to run the mile, which was four times around the track. Still, it was for my own good, working to build the endurance that's a necessary component for dream exercisers. Dreams don't manifest overnight but require time and patience to come into fruition.

Some days we feel like exercising; other days we don't. On days when we don't feel like exercising, we must make a choice to exercise even when we lack motivation. We must develop a habit or routine in exercising our dreams so we keep moving on days that we don't feel like it.

I don't consider myself a great athlete, but I do consider myself to be a great competitor. I remember back in college at Georgia Tech, I enrolled in a gymnastics class. Many of the routines were awkward to me. The still rings, pommel horse, and parallel bars required strong upper body muscles and coordination. I needed a good grade in the class, so I was determined not to be defeated. I was the guy who put a lot of heart into the routines. I just kept trying until I mastered each element to the best of my ability. I do remember making an "A" in the class. For me that was a dream come true. I think this class also motivated me to do well in my other classes and land on the Dean's List.

Exercising our dream options requires discipline, effort, and consistency. When we demonstrate our skills a few times, we become good at them, but when we can duplicate them many times, we become great at them. I'm still on the quest for six-pack abs and know that significant change will need to take place in my diet and exercise patterns for this dream to become reality.

Exercising is not just about what we do; it's also about what we refrain from doing. Discipline in exercising our dream options speaks to our self-control. Are we willing to give up something good to obtain something great? We all know that "good" is the enemy of "better" and "better" is the enemy of "best." The question is: which option must I exercise to achieve the best results?

In a race, no one competes for last place. In life, no one should live to stay in the same place his or her entire life. We are never too old to dream a new dream. We are never too unfit to improve our fitness level. It all begins in our mind and the ways we think about our future. What dream options do you need to begin exercising today?

Chapter 18

DREAM COMEBACKS

Everyone loves a good comeback story where an opponent is on the verge of defeat and time is running out. Out of nowhere, they find a way to score the winning touchdown, field goal, three-point shot or home run. The crowd goes wild.

Shani Davis was heavily favored to win a historic third consecutive gold medal at the 2014 Sochi Winter Olympics. He came away without a medal and was very disappointed. Two weeks later, Shani made a dream comeback by winning the gold medal at the ISU World Cup in Inzell, Germany, by defeating the Sochi gold medalist in the 1000-meters men's speed skating competition.

There will be times in our lives when we see our dreams defeated by circumstances we cannot control. It may be a temporary job layoff, a health challenge, or a loss of motivation. We must realize that delay is not denial and that failure is not final. If the desire to manifest our dream is great enough, we will do what it takes to make it happen.

In 2011, one of my clients, Loretta, had made plans for a dream vacation cruise with her family and friends. When it was time to make her final payment, she received news that her job was going away. As a result of this turn of events, she was forced to cancel her reservations and was not able to take this dream vacation. I'm sure she was disappointed by this misfortune. It may have been her turn to take a vacation, but it was not her time. Everything happens for a reason. According to Ecclesiastes 3:1, "To everything, there is a season." There is a time to dream and a time to manifest our dreams.

In March of 2014, I received a call from Loretta, expressing that she was ready to go on her cruise vacation. She had found another job in the field, which she enjoyed very much. I also discovered Loretta was unhappy in her previous job. Fate would have it that one door closed so that another one could be opened for her. In losing things that we don't need, we gain things that give purpose and meaning to our lives. There is a *kairos* moment for every purpose to be manifest in our lives. This is called our window of opportunity.

In manifesting our dreams, sometimes we must do unfulfilling things in order to get to a place of meaning and fulfillment. Dead-end jobs tend to hinder us from seeing and realizing our dreams. They also provide the pain we need to force us to make changes. Sometimes we change by our choice, and other times we change by force.

DREAM COMEBACKS   61

A dream setback is a dream setup for a dream comeback. Our dream may appear dead due to things we lack to bring it to manifestation. When we feel this way, we must look within, not without. Ralph Waldo Emerson said, "What lies behind us and what lies before us are tiny compared to what lies within us."

Greatness lies inside us. Everything we need to make a dream comeback is already within. Dead dreams can be resurrected. Dormant dreams can be awakened. Defeated dreams can be turned into dream comebacks!

Chapter 19

DREAM CHAMPIONS

Who are they? What do they accomplish? How do they achieve their goals?

Dream champions are strategists. They have a plan of attack when competing against their opposition. This game plan tells them what must be done to be successful. In a sport, such as basketball, it includes outscoring the opponent and limiting their opportunities to score. The enemies to our dreams must be subdued, defeated and dismantled.

Battles in life are about utilizing our strengths and weaknesses to compete against our adversaries. Dream champions know how to impose their strengths and exploit the weaknesses of the opponent.

It all comes down to the ability to perform under pressure.

Some people expand their potential while others shrink under pressure. Doing the hard things in life makes life easy, but doing the easy things in life makes life hard. Our ability to resist pressure increases our strengths, whereas buckling under pressure increases our weaknesses. Players who have traveled the path of greater resistance win most championships. Each round of competition gives strength for the next battle.

Dream champions are not intimidated by their opponents. Fear is not a part of their vocabulary. Courage is their mantra. They don't back up, they don't back down, and they don't back away. They push back, they fight back, and they come back, again and again. They may fall down but they do not stay down.

Champions rise to the occasion. When it's game time, it's time to play ball and play to win. How you play the game determines whether you win or lose. Champions play to win, whereas underachievers play to "not lose." This involves taking their skills and executing with effectiveness and consistency. Playing smart and not just playing hard wins championships.

A dream champion must develop an "all or nothing" attitude. We must bring our "A-game" to the table, look challengers in the face, and say, "Defeat me if you can." Our "A-game" is our game of attack, our game of attitude and our game of ability. When champions attack their dreams, their dreams move forward. There is dream advancement and dream momentum. There is dream progression with exponential growth.

As in basketball, each shot in the hoop adds points to the final score. An offensive attack displays dominance and control against the defense. If you can't stop your opponent from scoring points, you must be able to match them or settle for defeat.

Champions have a "take-charge attitude" when it's time to compete. They carry that aura of a winning presence. When they show up, they expect positive things to happen. They are inspired to win and inspire others through their winning performance. It's like the rush that you feel after the game is over. They make their fan base feel like a part of the victory.

The "A-game" also involves ability. If you are willing and able, you shall experience the reward of your labor. Some are willing but lack the ability, whereas some are capable but lack the will or motivation to execute their skills.

What motivates a champion? Sometimes it's a previous defeat. In Game 1 of the 2014 NBA finals, LeBron James, the star player for the Miami Heat, left the game with leg cramps in the fourth quarter, which resulted in a loss for his team. This loss motivated him to play inspiring basketball in the second game, which led to a win. Even the greatest players must have the will to win if they are to experience the greatness of their ability.

Another example of this motivation to execute was displayed by the San Antonio Spurs, who loss the 2013 championship in Game 7 and used this loss to propel them to the title in an impressive 4-1 series win in 2014. Their performance was a brilliant display of teamwork, talent and determination. The sting of defeat was transformed into the sweet taste of victory. It's time to think like a dream champion, perform like a dream champion, and win like a dream champion!

DREAM CHAMPIONS

Chapter 20

DREAM INVESTORS

"The future unfolds to those who are willing to manifest their dreams."

When I think of dream investors, I am reminded of all the people who shared their time, effort and experience to propel me to go to the "next level" of success in manifesting my dreams. I'd like to thank God for giving me the gift to write and the grace to endure hardship, adversity and opposition. Then there are my parents, who nurtured me and made great sacrifices so that I could attend one of the best high schools in Atlanta where I could receive deposits from great teachers who influenced my writing skills.

I have always loved writing; it was probably my first passion in life. Two of my favorite teachers with an impact on my writing and thinking were Ms. Bonnie Helget and Mr. James Robinson. They taught me how to improve an essay I wrote which won a $500 scholarship for being the best among all the students who competed that year. A great teacher understands that writing is important because it allows us to communicate our ideas and articulate our thoughts. All their teaching on grammar and proper sentence structure was an investment that pays out dividends as students become accomplished writers and authors.

I have learned many life lessons from teachers who paved the path for me to follow. In high school, I learned that writing was an art, so I could be creative. In college, I was instructed that writing is technical, so get to the point. As a writer, I strive to be creative and choose my words succinctly. I have learned that writing requires discipline of the mind, will and spirit. First, we must calm our inner selves long enough to hear what we are thinking. Next, we must sit down and capture our ideas on paper. We are all filled with expressive things to say but often lack the knowledge and motivation to write. My teachers taught me that writing can be fun as well as challenging. We must know what we are writing and write what we know.

Writing itself can be thought of as an investment in the lives of others. It feeds our imagination and opens our minds to new paradigms. There are many revelations and "aha" moments sparked by what we have to say. Have you ever read something and said, "You know, I never thought of it that way before?" According to Rabbi Shemuel ben Nachmani, "We do not see things as they are. We see them as we are."

DREAM INVESTORS   67

When I started blogging in 2014, one question that people often people often asked me was, "How do I get started?" Start with your passion. What are you passionate about? I love to travel, so I could share with you some of my many cruising experiences. It all starts with a dream. If you can dream it, you can manifest it. Live to manifest your dreams and life will be purposeful and fulfilling.

Life is not just about the destination but the experience along the journey. My journey is uniquely different from your journey, but we can learn from each other through our shared experiences of success as well as failure. The words I share today will pay dividends for future writers, dreamers, and achievers. Take time to invest in your personal best by creating the life that you desire. Our dreams are the blueprint to our future, so we must fuel them with our passion, potential, and possibilities.

Imagine what life would be like if we manifested all of our dreams. I'm sure it would be surreal and feel like we're actually dreaming.

Chapter 21

BUILDING YOUR DREAM TEAM

The best investment you can make towards manifesting your dreams is building your dream team. Manifesting your dreams requires investing in your dream team and divesting of your dream distractors. John Donne said, "No man is an island, entire of itself," and neither can you fully bring forth your dream without a dream team.

In chapter 12, I shared that the pearls on the dream team necklace must be compatible. Likewise, we must surround ourselves with like-minded individuals who want the best for us and are cheering us on to display the greatness that we have to offer the world.

When I was in 12th grade, I won an essay contest for writing about why I thought the birthday of the Rev. Martin Luther

King Jr. should become a national holiday. The teacher of the honors English class told her students that someone in her class should have won the contest. The truth is that I was capable of being in the honors class, but I chose not to be. This is not the type of person that you want on your dream team. Your dream team should only consist of people who celebrate your accomplishments. This teacher's comment should have been that the winner of the contest *should be* in her class.

When you win, the dream team wins! Individually, we can accomplish small things, but collectively we can accomplish great things. Your dream team is the fuel to your fire. They give you affirmation and encouragement when you doubt your confidence and ability to perform.

In identifying your dream team, seek people who are in motion and making things happen in their lives. A dream team that comes together with the same purpose in mind is unstoppable. Ecclesiastes 4:9 says, "Two are better than one, because they have a good reward for their labor." There is multiplied power in unity. There is power in agreement. When two or more are gathered together in the right place, at the right time with the same purpose, great things are manifested.

For the dream team, the word "can't" is not an option. Your dream team will help you find the way to make things happen in your life. They will help you think outside of the box and consider the options that are available to you. It's all about making connections and finding the resources that are available to you.

Your dream team believes in you and your dream. They believe in your desire to have the dream and your ability to manifest the dream. I found my dream team while surfing the internet. In 2014, I began writing "Manifesting Your Dreams," I needed motivation and direction to keep writing and complete the book. I was drawn to my Dream Coach, Dr. Alduan Tartt, who challenged me to take 100% responsibility for my life and make my dreams come true-- now!

This challenge resonated with my spirit and compelled me to commit to setting a deadline to complete the book. I accelerated my pace by setting writing goals to accomplish this mammoth task. Along this incredible journey, I knew my dream team was cheering for me and counting on me to cross the finish line.

When we embark on this type of pursuit of purpose with passion and persistence, we begin to see the separation of those who are our dream proponents from those who are dream opponents. We must understand that not everyone aspires to the same level of greatness our dream team does. Also, there are those who do not want us to make it to the top. When this happens, we must use these stumbling blocks as stepping-stones and keep climbing towards the apex of greatness.

Matthew 22:14 says, "Many are called but few are chosen." When we choose to follow our calling, we choose the path that leads to fulfillment and true identity. Those who are willing to risk the climate, weather the dream storms, and continue to climb will be among the chosen.

BUILDING YOUR DREAM TEAM

The dream team understands they are special. Each individual brings something unique and different to the team. Before I started writing today, I began cooking a pot of chili. Individually, the ingredients are simply corn, diced tomatoes, bell peppers, onions, veggie ground crumbles, salt, pepper, chili powder and tomato sauce. But when they are mixed together they begin to interact with each other and share their unique flavors with the other ingredients. They will evolve into a masterfully delicious tasting meal. On the dream team, ideas are shared and individual experiences are incorporated. Diverse backgrounds and a wealth of knowledge are available within the team. The learning curve is accelerated and the potential for unnecessary mistakes is reduced.

Proverbs 11:14 says, "In the multitude of counselors, there is safety." Your dream team is the ultimate mastermind to take brainstorming to its highest dimension. It's a meeting of the minds, an exchanging of ideas, a problem-solving session, and a time to make strategic plans to manifest your dreams.

If you're committed to your dream, divine appointment will guide you to the team. A Buddhist proverb says, "When the student is ready, the teacher will appear." When the dreamer is ready, the dream team will arise. Are you ready to manifest your dreams? This is your time! This is your moment! This is your season to manifest your dreams!

Milton Keynes UK
Ingram Content Group UK Ltd.
UKHW040704050124
435493UK00001B/211